Easy Learning Go

YANG HU

Simple is the beginning of wisdom. This book briefly explain the concept and vividly cultivate programming interest, this book for beginner fast learning Go programming.

http://en.verejava.com

ISBN: 9798639415234

CONTENTS

Go Installation

Download go1.14.2.windows-amd64.msi

https://golang.org/dl/
or
http://en.verejava.com/download.jsp?id=1

Double click go1.14.2.windows-amd64.msi **to start installation**

Click Next

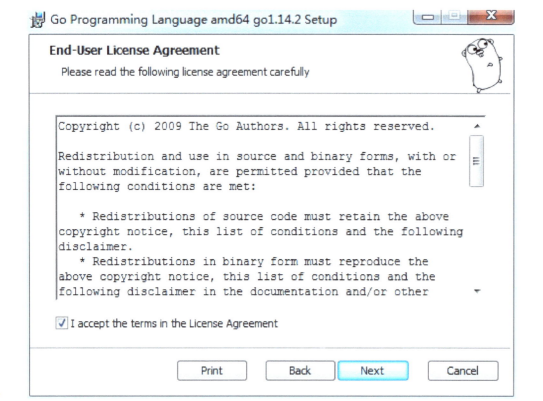

Click Next

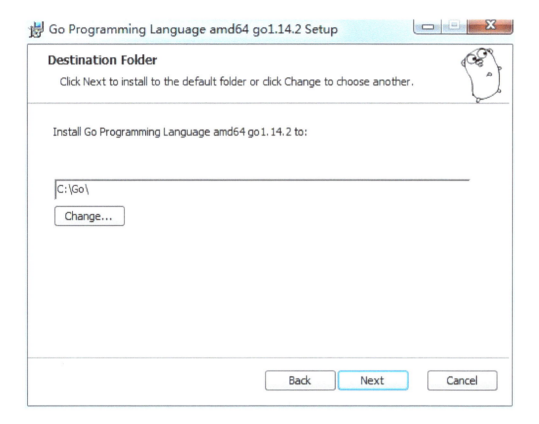

The Install directory: c:\Go   and then Click Next

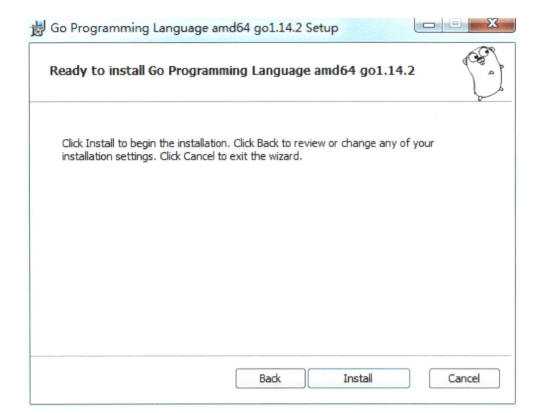

Click Install button

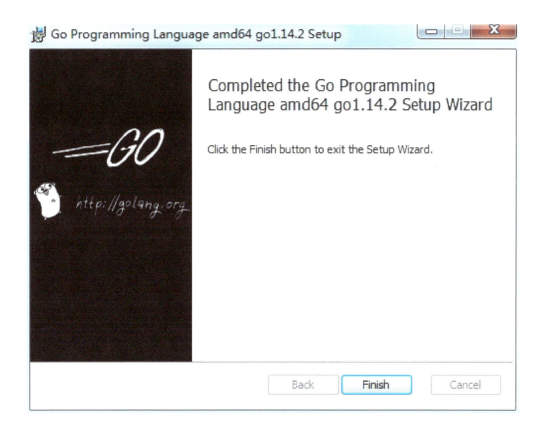

Click Finish Complete.

1. Create a working directory e:\Go

2. Create a go file : test.go in e:\Go

```go
package main

import "fmt"

func main() {
    fmt.Println("Hello, World!")
}
```

Open cmd window, change directory to e:\Go and then input go run test.go

Hello, World!

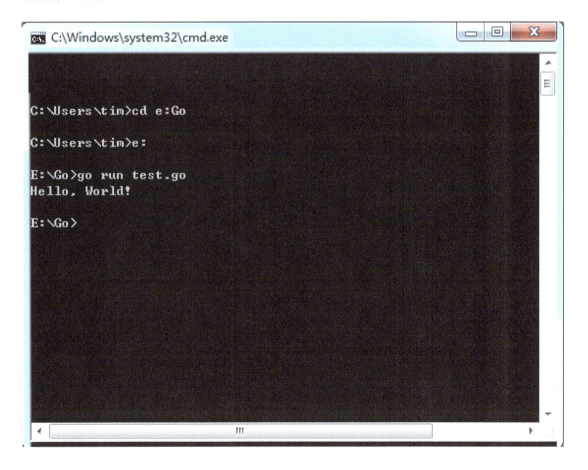

Hello World

Knowledge Tips

//:   single row comment
/*   */: multi row comment
fmt.Print(): Print content does not wrap a new line
fmt.Println(): Print content wrap a new line
package main: contains a package named main. represents an executable application
import "fmt": tells the Go compiler that this program needs to use the fmt package
func main(): is the entry function for program execution.

1. Create a go file : hello.go

```go
package main

import "fmt"

func main() {
    fmt.Print("A thousand miles ")
    fmt.Println("begins with a single step ")
    fmt.Println("Life is in time")
    fmt.Println("Today is life, now is the power")
}
```

Result:

A thousand miles begins with a single step
Life is in time
Today is life, now is the power

Variable

Variable : is a storage unit of a particular data type. You can give assign a name to this storage unit.

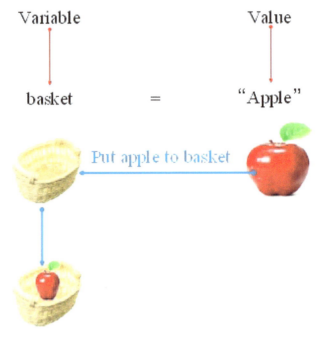

Knowledge Tips

Strings are defined between double quotes "..." like "Apple"

1.Create a go file : variable.go

```go
package main

import "fmt"

func main() {
    var basket = "Apple"
    fmt.Print(basket)
}
```

Result:

Apple

2.Change go file : variable.go replace "Apple" to "Orange"

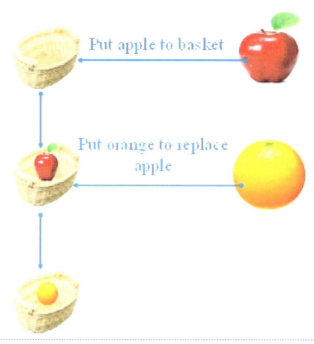

```go
package main

import "fmt"

func main() {
    var basket = "Apple"
    fmt.Println(basket)

    basket = "Orange"
    fmt.Println(basket)
}
```

Run Result:

Apple
Orange

Basic Data Type

Basic Data Type:

    1. integer: int
    2. float: float32, float64
    3. bool: can only be true, false
    4. string: " "

1.Create a go file : datatype.go

```go
package main

import "fmt"

func main() {
    var age int = 20

    var money float64 = 8000.0

    var word string = "waste time called imaginary"

    var married bool = true

    fmt.Println(age)
    fmt.Println(money)
    fmt.Println(word)
    fmt.Println(married)
}
```

Result:

20
8000.0
waste time called imaginary
True

Data Type Conversion

1.Create a go file : typeconvert.go

```go
package main

import "fmt"

func main() {

    var c1 int = 1
    var c2 float64 = 10.3
    // integer to float
    c2 = float64(c1)
    fmt.Println(c2)

    var d1 = 1
    var d2 = 10.3
    // float to integer requires conversion and may lose precision.
    d1=int(d2)
    fmt.Println(d1)

    //  + : concatenate two strings
    var str = "true agility is a very valuable thing"
    var str2 = str+", keep going"
    fmt.Println(str2)
}
```

Result:

```
1
10
true agility is a very valuable thing, keep going
```

Arithmetic Operator

Arithmetic operator:
   Add +, minus -, multiply *, divide /, take modulo %

1.Create a file : arithmetic.go

```go
package main
import "fmt"

func main() {

    var a = 1
    var b = 2
    var c = 3

    fmt.Println(a + b) # 3
    fmt.Println(a - b) # -1
    fmt.Println(a * b) # 2
    fmt.Println(b / a) # 2
    fmt.Println(c % b) # 1
}
```

Function

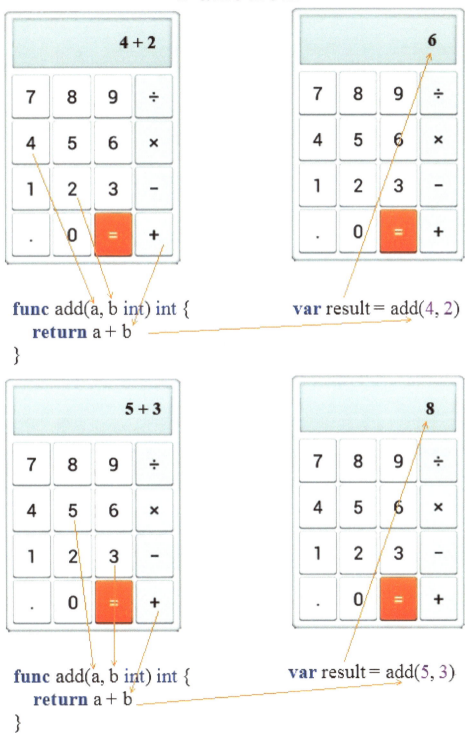

Function: is a block of code which only runs when it is called. You can pass data, known as parameters, into a function. can return data as a result.

Function Name	Parameter	Return Type	Return Value

```go
func add(a, b int) int {        var result = add(5, 3)
    return a + b
}
```

1.Create a file : function.go

```go
package main

import "fmt"

func add(a, b int) int {

    return a + b
}

func main() {

    var result = add(4, 2)
    fmt.Println(result) # 6

    result = add(5, 3)
    fmt.Println(result) # 8
}
```

2.Change file : function.go create 3 more functions about - , *, /

```go
package main
import "fmt"

func add(a, b int) int {
    return a + b
}

func sub(a, b int) int {
    return a - b
}

func multiply(a, b int) int {
    return a * b
}

func divide(a, b int) int {
    return a / b
}

func main() {

    var result = add(4, 2)
    fmt.Println(result) # 6

    result = sub(4, 2)
    fmt.Println(result) # 2

    result = multiply(4, 2)
    fmt.Println(result) # 8

    result = divide(4, 2)
    fmt.Println(result) # 2
}
```

Relational Operator

Relational operator: just only two value: true or false

1.Create a file : relational.go

```go
package main

import "fmt"

func main() {

	fmt.Println(100 > 200)
	fmt.Println(100 >= 100)
	fmt.Println(100 < 200)
	fmt.Println(100 <= 200)
	fmt.Println(100 == 100)
	fmt.Println(100 != 200)
}
```

Result:

false
true
true
true
true
true

Logical Operators

Logical Operators:
  and(&&), or(||), not(!)
  1. &&: return true if both sides of the operation are true, otherwise false
  2. || : return false when both sides of the operation are false, otherwise true
  3. !: if true return false, otherwise false return true

1.Create a file : logic.go

```go
package main
import "fmt"

func main() {

  fmt.Println(true && false)  // return false
  fmt.Println(false && true)  // return false
  fmt.Println(false && false) // return false
  fmt.Println(true && true)   // return true

  fmt.Println("--------------")

  fmt.Println(true || false)  // return true
  fmt.Println(false || true)  // return true
  fmt.Println(true || true)   // return true
  fmt.Println(false || false) // return false

  fmt.Println("--------------")

  fmt.Println(!true)  // return false
  fmt.Println(!false) // return true
}
```

2.Create a file : logic2.go

```go
package main

import "fmt"

func main() {

    fmt.Println(1 > 2 && 3 > 4) // return false
    fmt.Println(2 > 1 && 3 > 4) // return false

    fmt.Println("--------------")

    fmt.Println(2 > 1 || 3 > 4) // return true
    fmt.Println(2 > 1 || 3 > 4) // return true
    fmt.Println(1 > 2 || 3 > 4) // return true
}
```

Result:

```
false
false
--------------
true
true
false
```

If Conditional Statements

Simulation Games:
    if num equal 1: watermelon
    else if num equal 2: banana
    else: thunder

1.Create a file : If.go

```go
package main
import "fmt"

func main() {
  var num = 1
  if num == 1 {
    fmt.Println("You cut the watermelon")
  } else if num == 2 {
    fmt.Println("You cut the banana")
  } else {
    fmt.Println("You cut to the thunder")
  }
}
```

Result:
You cut the watermelon

If change num = 2 Run Result:
You cut the banana

Payroll tax example:
Tax amount = salary* tax rate
level:
500 -- 2000 $: 10% tax rate
2000--20000 $:   tax rate 20%
 More than 20000$:   tax rate 30%

2.Create a file : Tax.go

```go
package main

import "fmt"

func main() {

  var salary = 10000.0
  var tax = 0.0

  if salary >= 500 && salary < 2000 {
    tax = salary * 0.1
  } else if salary >= 2000 && salary < 20000 {
    tax = salary * 0.2
  } else {
    tax = salary * 0.3
  }

  fmt.Println(tax)
}
```

Result:

2000

Switch Statement

Airplane movement example:

Keyboard input a number 0, 1 , 2, 3

0 : Output The Airplane moves up

1 : Output The Airplane moves down

2 : Output The Airplane moves to the left

3 : Output The Airplane moves to the right

Otherwise the output does not move

Knowledge Tips

ifmt.Scanln(&num): Enter a string from the keyboard

2.Create a file : switchstatement.go

```go
package main
import "fmt"
func main() {
    var num int
    fmt.Println("keyboard enters a number 0: up, 1: down, 2: left, 3: right  ")
    fmt.Scanln(&num)
    switch num {
        case 0:
            fmt.Println("Airplane moves up")
        case 1:
            fmt.Println("Airplane moves down")
        case 2:
            fmt.Println("Airplane moves left")
        case 3:
            fmt.Println("Airplane moves right")
        default:
            fmt.Println("Airplane does not move")
    }
}
```

Result:

keyboard enters a number 0: up, 1: down, 2: left, 3: right

1

Airplane moves down

Run Again:

keyboard enters a number 0: up, 1: down, 2: left, 3: right

2

Airplane moves left

Run Again:

keyboard enters a number 0: up, 1: down, 2: left, 3: right

3

Airplane moves right

Run Again:

keyboard enters a number 0: up, 1: down, 2: left, 3: right

-1

Airplane does not move

For Loop

For Loop : allows code to be repeatedly executed.

```
for i := 0; i <= 10; i++ {        i=0   10 true executes the loop code
    fmt.Println(i)                    i++
}
```

```
for i := 0; i <= 10; i++ {        i=1   10 true executes the loop code
    fmt.Println(i)                    i++
}
```

```
for i := 0; i <= 10; i++ {        i=2   10 true executes the loop code
    fmt.Println(i)                    i++
}
```

Until i = 9

```
for i := 0; i <= 10; i++ {        i=9   10 true executes the loop code
    fmt.Println(i)                    i++
}
```

```
for i := 0; i <= 10; i++ {        i=10   10 False terminated
    fmt.Println(i)                    i++
}
```

For Loop is terminated

1.Create a file : ForLoop.go

```go
package main

import "fmt"

func main() {

    for i := 0; i <= 10; i++ {
        fmt.Println(i)
    }

}
```

Result:

0
1
2
3
4
5
6
7
8
9

For Loop Fruit Game

Simulation Games:

```
for {
    if num equal -1: break
    if num equal 1: watermelon
    else if num equal 2: banana
    else if num equal 3: peach
    else if num equal 0: thunder
}
```

1.Create a file : Game.go

```go
package main
import "fmt"
func main() {
    var num int
    for {
        if num == -1 { // If you enter -1 to terminate the game input
            break
        }

        fmt.Println("keyboard input 1: watermelon, 2: banana, 3: peach, 0: thunder  ")
        fmt.Scanln(&num)
        if num == 1 {
            fmt.Println("You cut the watermelon")
        } else if num == 2 {
            fmt.Println("You cut the banana")
        } else if num == 2 {
            fmt.Println("You cut the peach")
        } else if num == 0 {
            fmt.Println("You cut to the thunder, game termination")
        }
    }
}
```

Result:

```
C:\Users\tim\go\src\test\test.exe

keyboard input 1: watermelon, 2: banana, 3: peach, 0: thunder
1
You cut the watermelon
keyboard input 1: watermelon, 2: banana, 3: peach, 0: thunder
2
You cut the banana
keyboard input 1: watermelon, 2: banana, 3: peach, 0: thunder
3
keyboard input 1: watermelon, 2: banana, 3: peach, 0: thunder
0
You cut to the thunder, game termination
keyboard input 1: watermelon, 2: banana, 3: peach, 0: thunder
```

For Loop Bubble Ball

Bubble ball game:
 the game starts with 64 balls,
     requiring 8 balls per line. * is ball

1.Create a file : BallGame.go

```go
package main
import "fmt"

func main() {
   // range(1,65) == [1 -- 65)
   for i := 1; i < 65; i++ {
      fmt.Print("* ")
      if (i % 8) == 0 { // 8%8==0 , 16%8==0 , 24 %8==0, 32%8==0 , 48%8==0 , 64%8==0
         fmt.Println("") // wrap a new line
      }
   }
}
```

Result:
```
* * * * * * * *
* * * * * * * *
* * * * * * * *
* * * * * * * *
* * * * * * * *
* * * * * * * *
* * * * * * * *
* * * * * * * *
```

Continue and break

Knowledge Tips

strconv.Itoa: Convert integer to string

1.Create a file : ContinueBreak.go

```go
package main
import (
    "fmt"
    "strconv"
)

func main() {

    for i := 1; i < 65; i++ {
        if i == 13 {
            continue // current loop is not executed, continue to next the loop
        }

        if i == 20 {
            break // terminates and exit loop, jump out of loop
        }

        fmt.Print("*" + strconv.Itoa(i))

        if (i % 8) == 0 {
            fmt.Println("") // wrap a new line
        }
    }
}
```

Result:

```
*1 *2 *3 *4 *5 *6 *7 *8
*9 *10 *11 *12 *14 *15 *16
*17 *18 *19
```

Array

Array: is a numbered sequence of elements of a specific length.

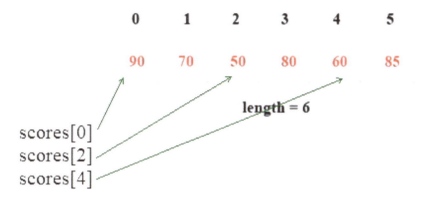

1. Create a file : one_array.go

```go
package main

import "fmt"

func main() {
    // the first index is 0, the second index is 1, and so on.
    var scores = [6]int{90, 70, 50, 80, 60, 85} // initial a array

    fmt.Println(scores[0])
    fmt.Println(scores[2])
    fmt.Println(scores[4])
}
```

Result:

90
50
60

Knowledge Tips

len(): function returns the number of items

2. Print all list scores one_array.go

```go
package main

import "fmt"

func main() {
    var scores = [...]int{90, 70, 50, 80, 60, 85}

    // Print all scores
    var length = len(scores)
    for i := 0; i < length; i++ {
        fmt.Println(scores[i])
    }

}
```

Result:

90
70
50
80
60
85

Two-Dimensional Array

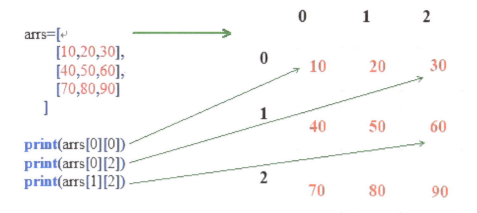

1. Create a file : two_array.go

```go
package main
import "fmt"

func main() {
  // define a two-dimensional list
  var arrs = [3][3]int{
    {10, 20, 30},
    {40, 50, 60},
    {70, 80, 90},
  }

  fmt.Println(arrs[0][0])
  fmt.Println(arrs[0][2])
  fmt.Println(arrs[1][2])
}
```

Result:

10
30
60

2. Print all value of Two-dimensional list two_array.go

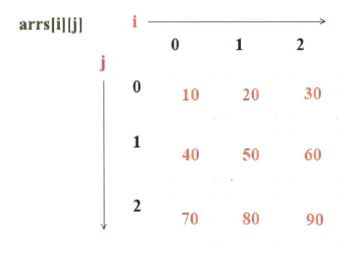

i: row index, j: column index

```go
package main
import "fmt"
func main() {
    var arrs = [3][3]int{
        {10, 20, 30},
        {40, 50, 60},
        {70, 80, 90},
    }
    var rowLength = len(arrs)      // count of rows
    var columnLength = len(arrs[0]) // count of columns

    // i is index of row and j is index of column
    for i := 0; i < rowLength; i++ {
        for j := 0; j < columnLength; j++ {
            fmt.Printf("%d,", arrs[i][j])
        }
        fmt.Println("")
    }
}
```

Result:
10 , 20 , 30 ,
40 , 50 , 60 ,
70 , 80 , 90 ,

34

Map

Map: is a collection of unordered pairs of key-value.

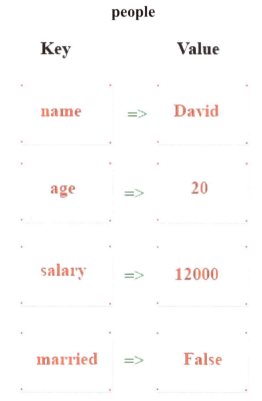

1. Create a file : testmap.go

```go
package main
import "fmt"

func main() {

	var people = map[string]string{"name": "David", "age": "20", "salary": "12000",
"married": "false"}

	// Print the value by key
	fmt.Println(people["name"])
	fmt.Println(people["age"])
	fmt.Println(people["salary"])
	fmt.Println(people["married"])

	fmt.Println("----------------------------")
	// Modify the elements in the map
	people["age"] = "25"
	people["salary"] = "18000"
	people["married"] = "true"
	fmt.Println(people)

	fmt.Println("----------------------------")
	// Delete element
	delete(people, "age")
	fmt.Println(people)
}
```

Result:

```
David
20
12000
false
----------------------------
map[age:25 married:true name:David salary:18000]
----------------------------
map[married:true name:David salary:18000]
```

Slice

Slice: is a dynamically-sized, flexible view into the elements of an array..

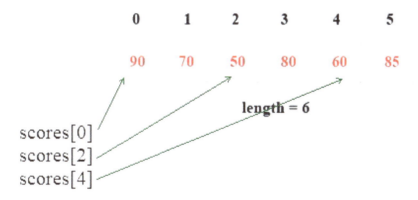

1. Create a file : slice.go

```go
package main

import "fmt"

func main() {

    // the first index is 0, the second index is 1, and so on.
    var scores = []int{90, 70, 50, 80, 60, 85} // initial a slice

    fmt.Println(scores[0])
    fmt.Println(scores[2])
    fmt.Println(scores[4])
}
```

Result:

90
50
60

Knowledge Tips

len(): function returns the number of items

2. Print all slice slice.go

```go
package main

import "fmt"

func main() {

    var scores = []int{90, 70, 50, 80, 60, 85}

    // Print all slice
    var length = len(scores)
    for i := 0; i < length; i++ {
        fmt.Println(scores[i])
    }
}
```

Result:

```
90
70
50
80
60
85
```

Knowledge Tips

append(): append new elements to a slice.

3. Append new elements to a slice. slice.go

```go
package main

import "fmt"

func main() {

    var scores = []int{90, 70, 50, 80, 60, 85}

    scores = append(scores, 100)
    scores = append(scores, 200)

    // Print all slice
    var length = len(scores)
    for i := 0; i < length; i++ {
        fmt.Printf("%d,", scores[i])
    }

}
```

Result:

90,70,50,80,60,85,100,200,

4. Cut slice to sub slice. slice.go

```go
package main

import "fmt"

func main() {

    var scores = []int{90, 70, 50, 80, 60, 85}

    fmt.Println(scores[1:3]) // cut slice index from 1 to 3
    fmt.Println(scores[:3])  // cut slice index from 0 to 3
    fmt.Println(scores[3:])  // cut slice index from 3 to end

}
```

Result:

```
[70 50]
[90 70 50]
[80 60 85]
```

Range

Range: form of the for loop iterates over a slice or map.

1. loop iterates over a slice in range.go

```go
package main

import "fmt"

func main() {

    var scores = []int{90, 70, 50, 80, 60, 85}

    // Print all slice
    for _, score := range scores {
        fmt.Println(score)
    }

}
```

Result:

```
90
70
50
80
60
85
```

2. loop iterates over a map in range.go

```go
package main

import "fmt"

func main() {

    var people = map[string]string{"name": "David", "age": "20", "salary": "12000", "married": "false"}

    for key, value := range people {
        fmt.Printf("%s -> %s\n", key, value)
    }

}
```

Result:

```
salary -> 12000
married -> false
name -> David
age -> 20
```

Struct

struct: are typed collections of fields.

1. Create a file : struct_app.go

```go
package main

import "fmt"

type Book struct {

    title  string
    author string
}

func main() {

    // create a book1 struct
    var book1 = Book{"Easy Learning Go", "Yang Hu"}

    // print struct member
    fmt.Println(book1.title)
    fmt.Println(book1.author)

}
```

Result:

Easy Learning Go
Yang Hu

2. Create struct slice in struct_app.go

```go
package main

import "fmt"

type Book struct {
  title  string
  author string
}

func main() {

  // create a  struct slice
  var bookSlice = []Book{}

  bookSlice = append(bookSlice, Book{"Easy Learning Go", "Yang Hu"})
  bookSlice = append(bookSlice, Book{"Easy Learning Java", "Tim"})
  bookSlice = append(bookSlice, Book{"Easy Learning Javascript", "Timothy"})
  bookSlice = append(bookSlice, Book{"Easy Learning Python 3", "Joseph"})

  // Print all slice
  var length = len(bookSlice)
  for i := 0; i < length; i++ {
    var book = bookSlice[i]
    fmt.Printf(book.title + " , " + book.author + " \n")
  }

}
```

Result:

Easy Learning Go , Yang Hu
Easy Learning Java , Tim
Easy Learning Javascript , Timothy
Easy Learning Python 3 , Joseph

3. Create struct map in struct_app.go

```go
package main

import "fmt"

type Book struct {

    title  string
    author string
}

func main() {

    // create a  struct map
    var bookMap = map[string]Book{}

    bookMap["book1"] = Book{"Easy Learning Go", "Yang Hu"}
    bookMap["book2"] = Book{"Easy Learning Javascript", "Timothy"}

    var book1 = bookMap["book1"]
    fmt.Println(book1)

    var book2 = bookMap["book2"]
    fmt.Println(book2)

}
```

Result:

{Easy Learning Go Yang Hu}
{Easy Learning Javascript Timothy}

Interface

interface: are named collections of method signatures..

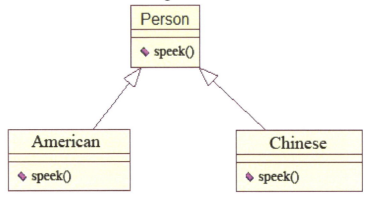

1. Create a file : interface_app.go

```go
package main
import "fmt"

type Person interface {
   speek()
}

type American struct {
}

func (american American) speek() {
   fmt.Println("I speek english")
}

type Chinese struct {
}

func (chinese Chinese) speek() {
   fmt.Println("I speek chinese")
}
```

```
func main() {
    var person Person

    person = new(American)
    person.speek()

    person = new(Chinese)
    person.speek()
}
```

Result:

I speek english
I speek Chinese

Pointer

Each variable has a memory address, & represents the address of the variable in memory.

	age	price	name
Adress :	c00000a1c8	c00000a1e0	c0000321f0

1. Create a file : pointer.go

```go
package main

import "fmt"

func main() {

    var age int
    var price float64
    var name string

    // & Get the storage address of the variable
    fmt.Printf("age address : %x\n", &age)
    fmt.Printf("price address : %x\n", &price)
    fmt.Printf("name address : %x\n", &name)

}
```

Result:

```
age address :   c00000a1c8
price address :   c00000a1e0
name address :   c0000321f0
```

2. A pointer is a variable whose value is the address of another variable.

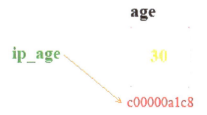

```go
package main

import "fmt"

func main() {

    var age int = 30
    var ip_age *int // Declare integer pointer variables

    ip_age = &age
    fmt.Printf("ip_age address : %x\n", ip_age)
    fmt.Printf("ip_age value : %d\n", *ip_age)

}
```

Result:

ip_age address :   c00000a1c8
ip_age value :   30

3. Pointer Array in pointer.go

```go
package main

import "fmt"

const MAXSIZE int = 3

func main() {

    var scores = []int{80, 90, 100}
    var i int
    var p [MAXSIZE]*int

    for i := 0; i < MAXSIZE; i++ {
        p[i] = &scores[i] //Assign  address to pointer array
    }

    for i = 0; i < MAXSIZE; i++ {
        fmt.Printf("scores[%d] = %d\n", i, *p[i])
    }

}
```

Result:

scores[0] = 80
scores[1] = 90
scores[2] = 100

Go Concurrency

Concurrency is an ability of a program to do multiple things at the same time. This means a program that have two or more tasks that run individually of each other, at about the same time, but remain part of the same program.

Car and train running at the same time

1. Create a file : concurrency.go

```go
package main

import (
    "fmt"
    "time"
)

func run(str string) {
    for i := 0; i < 4; i++ {
        time.Sleep(500 * time.Millisecond)
        fmt.Printf("%s goroutine run %d \n", str, i)
    }
}

func main() {
    go run("Car") //start a new goroutine
    run("Train")
}
```

Result:

Car goroutine run 0
Train goroutine run 0
Train goroutine run 1
Car goroutine run 1
Car goroutine run 2
Train goroutine run 2
Train goroutine run 3
Car goroutine run 3

Car goroutine and Train goroutine are executed alternately

Knowledge Tips

Sync.WaitGroup: from sync package is used to wait till two non-main goroutines terminate. Otherwise there wouldn't any guarantee that any of those goroutines would even start.

sync.Mutex: is used to provide a locking mechanism to ensure that only one Goroutine is running the critical section of code at any point of time to prevent race condition from happening. Mutex is available in the sync package. There are two methods defined on Mutex namely Lock and Unlock

2. goroutine synchronization in concurrency.go

```go
package main

import (
    "fmt"
    "sync"
    "time"
)

var lock sync.Mutex
var wg sync.WaitGroup

func run(str string) {
    lock.Lock()
    for i := 0; i < 4; i++ {
        time.Sleep(500 * time.Millisecond)
        fmt.Printf("%s goroutine run %d \n", str, i)
    }
    lock.Unlock()
    wg.Done()//goroutine count -- in WaitGroup
}

func main() {
    wg.Add(2) // add 2 goroutine to WaitGroup goroutine count=2
    go run("Car")
    go run("Train")
    wg.Wait()// waiting until goroutine count==0
}
```

Result:

Car goroutine run 0
Car goroutine run 1
Car goroutine run 2
Car goroutine run 3
Train goroutine run 0
Train goroutine run 1
Train goroutine run 2
Train goroutine run 3

When Car goroutine lock (), Train goroutine must wait, When Car goroutine unlock ()
Train goroutine can execute

Channel

Channels: are the pipes that connect concurrent goroutines. You can send values into channels from one goroutine and receive those values into another goroutine.

Knowledge Tips

Channel Buffer: By default channels are unbuffered, meaning that they will only accept sends (chan <-) if there is a corresponding receive (<- chan) ready to receive the sent value. Buffered channels accept a limited number of values without a corresponding receiver for those values.

make(chan val-type): Create a new channel.
make(chan val-type, buffSize): Create a new channel specify the buffer size.
channel <- syntax: Send a value into a channel.
msg <-channel syntax: receives a value from the channel.

1. Create a file : channel.go

```go
package main
import "fmt"

var messages = make(chan string)
var msg string

func sendMessage() {
  messages <- "Good"
  messages <- "Morning "
}

func main() {
  go sendMessage()

  msg = <-messages //receive message
  fmt.Println(msg)

  msg = <-messages //receive message
  fmt.Println(msg)
}
```

Result:
Good
Morning

2. Go traverse channel and close channel in channel.go

```go
package main

import (
    "fmt"
    "strconv"
)

var messages = make(chan string)
var msg string

func sendMessage() {
    for i := 0; i < 5; i++ {
        messages <- "message " + strconv.Itoa(i)
    }
    close(messages)
}

func main() {

    go sendMessage()

    for msg := range messages {
        fmt.Println(msg)
    }
}
```

Result:

message 0
message 1
message 2
message 3
message 4

File

Go Language can use **ioutil** read file

Create a data file: data.txt

Love is patient, love is kind. It always protects, always trusts, always hopes, always perseveres. Love never fails.

1. Create fileread.go

```go
package main

import (
    "fmt"
    "io/ioutil"
)

func main() {

    data, err := ioutil.ReadFile("data.txt") // data is slice of byte

    if err != nil {
        fmt.Println("File reading error", err)
    }

    fmt.Println(string(data))
}
```

2. ioutil write content to file

Create filewrite.go

```go
package main

import (
    "io/ioutil"
)

func main() {

    content := "Love never fails. "
    ioutil.WriteFile("data.txt", []byte(content), 0777) // 0777 file authorization

}
```

Result:
data.txt

Love never fails.

3. os read file

func OpenFile(name string, flag int, perm FileMode)

flag:
os.O_WRONLY | os.O_CREATE | O_EXCL // If it already exists, it fails
os.O_WRONLY | os.O_CREATE // If it already exists, it will overwrite, not clear the original file, but directly overwrite
os.O_WRONLY | os.O_CREATE | os.O_APPEND // If it already exists, append at the end

Create a data file: data.txt

Love is patient, love is kind. It always protects, always trusts, always hopes, always perseveres. Love never fails.

Create fileread.go

```go
package main
import (
    "fmt"
    _ "io/ioutil"
    "os"
)

func main() {
    f, _ := os.OpenFile("data.txt", os.O_RDWR|os.O_APPEND, 0777)
    defer f.Close()

    data := make([]byte, 10) //only store 10 byte
    count, err := f.Read(data)

    if err != nil {
        fmt.Println(err)
    }

    fmt.Print(string(data[:count]))
}
```

Result:

love is pa

4. os loop read file append to slice

Create a data file: data.txt

Love is patient, love is kind. It always protects, always trusts, always hopes, always perseveres. Love never fails.

Create fileread.go

```go
package main
import (
    "fmt"
    _ "io/ioutil"
    "os"
)

func main() {
    f, _ := os.OpenFile("data.txt", os.O_RDWR|os.O_APPEND, 0777)
    defer f.Close()

    data := make([]byte, 10) //only store 10 byte
    var dataSlice = []string{}

    for {
        count, err := f.Read(data)
        if count <= 0 {
            break
        }
        if err != nil {
            fmt.Println(err)
        }
        dataSlice = append(dataSlice, string(data[:count]))
    }
    fmt.Print(dataSlice)
}
```

Result:

[Love is pa tient, lov e is kind. It always protects, always tr usts, alwa ys hopes, always per severes. L ove never fails.]

5. os loop read file line by line

Create a data file: data.txt

Love is patient,
love is kind.
It always protects,
always trusts,
always hopes,
always perseveres.
Love never fails.

Create fileread.go

```go
package main
import (
    "bufio"
    "fmt"
    "log"
    "os"
)

func main() {
    f, err := os.Open("data.txt")
    if err != nil {
        log.Fatal(err)
    }

    s := bufio.NewScanner(f)
    for s.Scan() {
        fmt.Println(s.Text())
    }
}
```

Result:
Love is patient,
love is kind.
 It always protects,
always trusts,
always hopes,
always perseveres.
Love never fails.

6. Multi goroutine read file

Create a data file: data.txt

> Love is patient, love is kind. It always protects, always trusts, always hopes

```go
info, _ := os.Stat(fileName)
size := info.Size()
var goroutineFileSize int64
var goroutineCount int64 = 3    Shard size

if size%goroutineCount == 0 {
    goroutineFileSize = size / goroutineCount
} else {
    goroutineFileSize = size / goroutineCount
    goroutineCount++
}
```

Total Size

data.txt

```
Love is patient, love is kind. It always protects, always trusts, always hopes
```

Shard Position

```go
func readFile(sfile *os.File, i int, goroutineFileSize int64) {
    b := make([]byte, goroutineFileSize)
    sfile.Seek(int64(i)*goroutineFileSize, 0)
    sfile.Read(b)
    mapFile[i] = string(b)
    wg.Done()
}
```

Create fileread.go

```go
package main
import (
  "fmt"
  "os"
  "sync"
)
var wg sync.WaitGroup
var mapFile = map[int]string{}

func main() {
  fileName := "data.txt"
  sfile, err := os.Open(fileName)
  if err != nil {
    fmt.Println(nil)
  }

  info, _ := os.Stat(fileName)
  size := info.Size()
  var goroutineFileSize int64
  var goroutineCount int64 = 3
  if size%goroutineCount == 0 {
    goroutineFileSize = size / goroutineCount
  } else {
    goroutineFileSize = size / goroutineCount
    goroutineCount++
  }

  fmt.Printf("File Total : %v \n", size)
  fmt.Printf("Goroutine Count : %v \n", goroutineCount)
  fmt.Printf("Goroutine File Size : %v \n", goroutineFileSize)

  wg.Add(int(goroutineCount))
  for i := 0; i < int(goroutineCount); i++ {
    go readFile(sfile, i, goroutineFileSize)
  }
  wg.Wait()

  for key, value := range mapFile {
    fmt.Printf("%s -> %s\n", key, value)
  }
  defer sfile.Close()
```

```
}

func readFile(sfile *os.File, i int, goroutineFileSize int64) {
    b := make([]byte, goroutineFileSize)
    sfile.Seek(int64(i)*goroutineFileSize, 0)
    sfile.Read(b)
    mapFile[i] = string(b)
    wg.Done()
}
```

Result:

File Total： 78
Goroutine Count： 3
Goroutine File Size： 26
%!s(int=0) -> Love is patient, love is k
%!s(int=1) -> ind. It always protects, a
%!s(int=2) -> lways trusts, always hopes

Thanks for learning, if you want to learn web coding, please study book

http://en.verejava.com

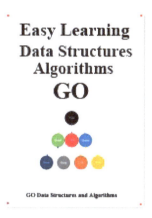

If you enjoyed this book and found some benefit in reading this, I'd like to hear from you and hope that you could take some time to post a review on Amazon. Your feedback and support will help us to greatly improve in future and make this book even better.

You can follow this link now.

http://www.amazon.com/review/create-review?&asin=B087H9JZVC

Different country reviews only need to modify the amazon domain name in the link:
www.amazon.co.uk
www.amazon.de
www.amazon.fr
www.amazon.es
www.amazon.it
www.amazon.ca
www.amazon.nl
www.amazon.in
www.amazon.co.jp
www.amazon.com.br
www.amazon.com.mx
www.amazon.com.au

I wish you all the best in your future success!